EXPLORING LIFE CYCLES

Butterflies

Aaron Carr

AV2

www.av2books.com

Step 1
Go to **www.av2books.com**

Step 2
Enter this unique code

FOWIX7DZG

Step 3
Explore your interactive eBook!

EXPLORING LIFE CYCLES

Butterflies

Start!

AV2 is optimized for use on any device

Your interactive eBook comes with...

Read

Audio
Listen to the entire book read aloud

Videos
Watch informative video clips

Weblinks
Gain additional information for research

Try This!
Complete activities and hands-on experiments

Key Words
Study vocabulary, and complete a matching word activity

Quizzes
Test your knowledge

Slideshows
View images and captions

View new titles and product videos at
www.av2books.com

Butterflies

CONTENTS

EXPLORING LIFE CYCLES

All animals begin life, grow, and make more animals.

This is a life cycle.

Butterflies are **insects**.

Insects have **three-part** bodies.

An insect has antennae on its head.

Butterflies are born when they hatch from eggs.

Baby butterflies are called caterpillars.

This is the larva stage of their life cycle.

Caterpillars eat a lot.
They grow very fast.

Caterpillars drop their skin when they grow too big for it. This is called shedding.

A caterpillar sticks itself to a **branch** when it is fully grown.

The caterpillar's skin turns into a hard shell. The shell is called a chrysalis.

This is the pupa stage of the life cycle.

A caterpillar may stay inside its chrysalis for months.

It changes into a butterfly inside its shell.

A butterfly is fully grown when it comes out of its shell.

Its four wings start out soft. They soon turn hard.

Butterflies can **fly** after a few hours.

This is the **imago stage** of their life cycle.

Butterflies lay eggs soon after they start to fly. They stick their eggs to leaves with a special glue.

Butterfly eggs may be round, oval, or tube-shaped.

There are about
20,000 kinds
of butterflies.

Each kind is a
different size
or color.

The color and size of a butterfly come from its **parents**.

Life Cycles Quiz

A butterfly's life cycle has four stages.

Larva Pupa

Adult Egg

Which **stage** of the life cycle do you see in each picture?

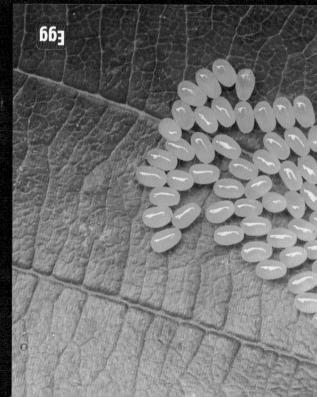

Egg

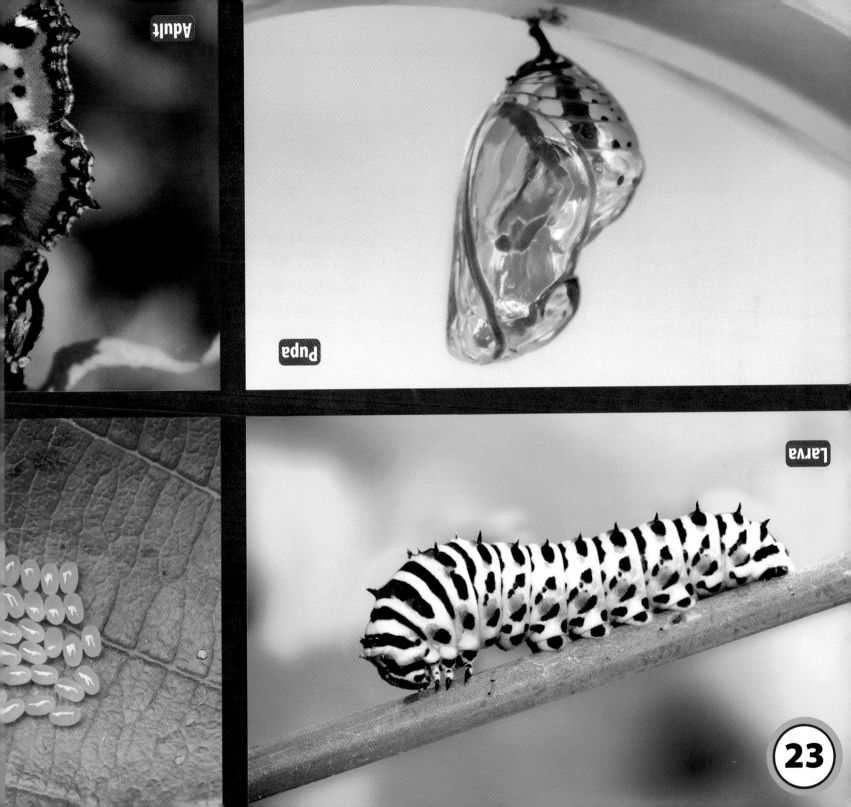

Adult

Pupa

Larva

23

KEY WORDS

Research has shown that as much as 65 percent of all written material published in English is made up of 300 words. These 300 words cannot be taught using pictures or learned by sounding them out. They must be recognized by sight. This book contains 60 common sight words to help young readers improve their reading fluency and comprehension. This book also teaches young readers several important content words, such as proper nouns. These words are paired with pictures to aid in learning and improve understanding.

Page	Sight Words First Appearance
4	a, all, and, animals, grow, is, life, make, more, this
6	are, have, part, three
7	an, has, head, its, on
8	from, they, when
9	of, the, their
10	eat, very
11	big, for, it, too
12	to
13	hard, into, turns
15	changes, may
16	comes, four, out, soon, start
17	after, can, few
18	leaves, with
19	be, or
20	about, different, each, kinds, there
22	do, in, picture, see, which, you

Page	Content Words First Appearance
4	life cycle
6	bodies, butterflies, insects
7	antenna
8	eggs
9	caterpillars, larva stage
11	shedding, skin
12	branch
13	chrysalis, pupa stage, shell
15	months
16	wings
17	hours, imago stage
18	glue
20	color, size
21	parents

Published by AV2
350 5th Avenue, 59th Floor New York, NY 10118
Website: www.av2books.com

Library of Congress Cataloging-in-Publication Data
Names: Carr, Aaron, author.
Title: Butterflies / Aaron Carr.
Description: New York, NY : AV2, [2021] | Series: Exploring life cycles |
  Audience: Ages 4-8 | Audience: Grades K-1
Identifiers: LCCN 2020011799 (print) | LCCN 2020011800 (ebook) | ISBN
  9781791127046 (library binding) | ISBN 9781791127053 (paperback) | ISBN
  9781791127060 | ISBN 9781791127077
Subjects: LCSH: Butterflies--Juvenile literature.

Classification: LCC QL544.2 .C366 2021 (print) | LCC QL544.2 (ebook) |
  DDC 595.78/9--dc23
LC record available at https://lccn.loc.gov/2020011799
LC ebook record available at https://lccn.loc.gov/2020011800

Printed in Guangzhou, China
1 2 3 4 5 6 7 8 9 0 24 23 22 21 20

042020
100919

Art Director: Terry Paulhus Project Coordinator: John Willis

Every reasonable effort has been made to trace ownership and to obtain permission to reprint copyright material. The publisher would be pleased to have any errors or omissions brought to its attention so that they may be corrected in subsequent printings.

The publisher acknowledges Getty Images and iStock as the primary image suppliers for this title.